SCIENCE

Lord Loveday Ememe

SCIENCE

Lord Loveday Ememe

SCIENCE

By Lord Loveday Ememe and available from Lulu and Amazon

The constitution and policing

Heresy

Starfleet

The Supernatural

Creation

Deterrence

Stalking

The media

Adam

Criminal Responsibility

The Wicked

Common Law

Racism

Regulation

SCIENCE

www.lulu.com

Copyright © Lord Loveday Ememe 2017

The author asserts the moral right to be recognized as the author of this work
ISBN: 978-1-326-91581-0

SCIENCE

Table of Contents

1 What is science?

2 Social science

3 The supernatural unscientific constitution

4 The civil scientific constitution

5 Author's notes

6 Author's biography

7 Bibliography

SCIENCE

SCIENCE

What is science?

Lord Loveday Ememe

SCIENCE

Science is a concept or service for the benefit of man, it is used as an aid in the establishment, and maintenance of a civilization and it is used to give order to disorder, to build and to regulate, establishing civilized behaviour.

Science has always existed; it existed before the creation of man, Lord Adam, according to the Christian teachings. It existed in the form of the Garden of Eden which can be referred to as the science of Eden. Lord Adam in the Garden of Eden was the representation of the civil noble constitution.

Science was always intended for good purposes to meet the needs of the delicate nature of the civil noble scientific constitution.

Science is used as a method to provide goods and services for the civil noble lord, the goods, and services must satisfy the criteria for safety, durability, accessibility, and usability using the civil noble lord as the standard. Goods and services that do not meet the required standard but presented as if they do, are for the uncivilized supernatural unscientific constitution pretending unlawfully to be the civil noble scientific constitution.

The rights and privileges of the civil noble lord and the protocols for contact and communication with the civil noble lord are scientific methods for regulating supernatural beings that establishes law and order.

Science is used as a mechanism to provide information, education, security in the form of a police service, housing, transportation, for communication etcetera, using the civil

SCIENCE

noble lord as the standard, and as a method or mechanism acting and lying are not required or necessary.

The scientific method for regulating supernatural beings, the civil rights and privileges of the civil noble lord and protocols for contact and communication with the civil noble lord, applies to all supernatural beings regardless of what type of relationship they believe they have with the civil noble lord. It is based on this that there is a requirement of impartiality from police officers while carrying out their duties. It is what it is modelled on.

Social interaction might appear to be impossible for supernatural beings, without acting or lying, on the contrary, scientific interaction with the science of language is possible with self-control, respecting another being's right to privacy regardless of what you think you know. It is an individual right to disclose personal information. Exceptions to this are commissions of crimes, when the need for the safety of the public outweighs the individual rights of the individual, for the criminally responsible.

Science is orderliness, it is meant to be applied for good purposes, it regulates, and exposes lawlessness, and it as a consequence has been sabotaged by the treachery of the wicked.

The scientific formula for the creation of the police service requires the consent or commissioning of the civil noble lord in order for the police service to be used for only good purposes. As a consequence the consent or commissioning cannot be forced or absent in a police service. This is the

SCIENCE

reason the consent or commissioning can only be obtained by meeting the sacred condition of the official scientific confirmation of the civil noble lord as commissioner of police, the supreme commander, the standard. This is to make sure that the civil noble lord is not vulnerable to supernatural political manipulations or puppetism. Unfortunately, science is being misapplied by the unscientific supernatural beings for political purposes, unguided by science or the law; supernatural beings are criminally insane, destructive, and unsociable.

Science is the good, simple to understand or understandable, to understand means to have some sort of form, tangible. The complex on the other hand, means bad, unintelligible, not understandable, and unscientific. Unscientific means non-existence. The standard for comprehensibility is the civil noble scientific constitution.

Parenting is the completion of the scientific process of creating life, the law is the main component of parenting, and parents that do not have a proper understanding of the law or do not apply the law correctly while parenting are criminally insane given the nature of the supernatural constitution. The law is very strict with the acceptance of relationships between the civil and supernatural constitutions because of the hostile nature of the supernatural constitution. The law makes the determination that the civil noble lord is born of God, God means the law, which confirms that regardless of who the supernatural being is, they are required to be law abiding in order not to be

SCIENCE

threats to the civil noble lord given the hostile nature of the supernatural constitution.

All the civil rights and privileges of the civil noble lord and the protocols for contact and communication with the civil noble lord form the legal framework or scientific process for the establishment of the state that regulates supernatural beings.

Science has been redefined or misapplied for purposes of total anarchy that caters to the nature of the wicked, supernatural beings. It is being used to create weapons of destruction, supernatural phenomena referred to as diseases or illnesses, supernatural phenomena referred to as thunderstorms, hurricanes, tornadoes, old age or ageing, death etcetera. These supernatural attacks have been conveniently referred to as natural scientific occurrences, compromising the sacred purpose of science. Some argue that these supernatural phenomena are punishments, but the state requires that punishments are done in an orderly scientific way so that law abiding citizens are not affected or inconvenienced. There has to be judgement and a clearly defined purpose for punishments, which should only affect the criminally responsible, supernatural beings.

Supernatural beings take for granted the toxic unfriendly nature of the supernatural constitution, the scientific methods of legal processes or procedures and domestic and international legislations that recognizes only the civil noble constitution do not take for granted the toxic unfriendly nature of the supernatural constitution, by recognizing only the civil noble constitution, give the legal person authority over the supernatural constitution. When dealing with the civil noble lord under any legal process or legislation, the legal process or legislation becomes real, active, and not role play when only supernatural beings are involved. The only relevant being is the civil legal being whose communications can only be taken as orders or commands because by law the legal being has authority over any other being not legally recognized. For supernatural beings to pretend to be legal beings under any legal process or legislation when dealing with the civil noble lord, is to lie, categorized by common law as casting spells on the civil noble lord. Supernatural beings use their unscientific illegal supernatural peers as the standard or measure to determine their friendliness or sociability which is misleading because the legal scientific standard for determining sociability is the civil legal scientific constitution.

Unfortunately, supernatural beings while unlawfully pretending to be legal beings under legislations, legal processes or procedures while dealing with real legal beings behave supernaturally, bugging, rather than scientifically causing mental and physical harm.

The state is a police service, the monarchy in the United Kingdom and other monarchies around the world although meant to represent the correct identification, interpretation and application of the Christian teachings, the law, under the leadership of the real ruler, the civil noble lord, are ancient types of police services. The police service in the United

SCIENCE

Kingdom, the metropolitan police service, which is how the United Nations is meant to operate under the leadership of the civil noble lord when operating correctly without political influence is the modern scientific advancement or improvement of the ancient style police service, the monarchy.

Science unlike the supernatural represents safety, it is meant to be used for good purposes, and it does not require worship to gain access to goods and services. The magnitude of lawlessness by supernatural beings has resulted in the compromise of the concept of science, making science unlawfully supernatural eliminating the necessary checks and balances, law and order. The elimination of the safety and independence of science makes everything including legal rights political subject to the goodwill of the wicked, supernatural beings.

The civil noble constitution is within the boundaries of science, making the civil noble lord safe and legal, not criminally responsible. Science is used to bridge the gap between the civil and supernatural constitutions which is meant to facilitate the establishment of the state. To undermine science is to undermine the state leading to the establishment of hell, organized barbarism that caters to the wicked nature of the supernatural constitution. Some argue that the needs of the many outweigh the needs of the few making lawlessness lawful, the proper interpretation of the needs of the many is the safe, lawful and universal. Everyone, civil and supernatural beings, can survive and live peacefully

SCIENCE

in conditions that are lawful that use the civil noble lord as the standard, which makes the civil constitution universal, non-discriminatory.

Science is being undermined with the healthcare provisions in place for the civil noble lord, technology should be in place to counteract any type of supernatural attack referred to as illness or disease. Healthcare provisions at present are inadequate, inhumane, butchery referred to as surgery that caters to the hostile, sadistic nature of the supernatural constitution.

Science unfortunately is being used as a weapon by demons for supernatural attacks they refer to as natural occurrences like hurricanes, thunderstorms, cobwebs, mould, mildew, mycelium, earthquakes, tornadoes, diseases or illnesses, ageing, death etcetera. They are gradually terraforming the planet to suit the toxic nature of the supernatural constitution at the expense of the wellbeing or the peace of the vulnerable, including the peace of the civil noble lord. These phenomena do not fit into the category of the scientific or natural occurrences because they are threatening to the civil noble lord who is the standard or determinant. They are unscientific supernatural phenomena being referred to as scientific natural occurrences by the wicked as a consequence of the flaw in the demonic constitution, a real illness, referred to as dumb criminal syndrome.

The civil noble constitution, whose constitution is within the boundaries of science, as a consequence legal and safe, is by

SCIENCE

sacred determination overlord. Common law, the bible, states that the civil constitution has dominion over the planet. This simply means that the civil scientific constitution is the standard for universal application. Supernatural beings have tried to model themselves on the civil noble lord by acquiring land by one type of force or the other to gain the status of a lord. This was done for power tripping purposes to dominate their peers, political rather than legal, without the understanding of the definition or purpose of a ruler.

For supernatural beings to be scientific, they have to be regulated under the governance of the civil scientific lord as overlord. It serves no useful purpose to manipulate this sacred requirement with the misuse of supernatural powers and senses to use the civil noble lord as a puppet to maintain lawlessness.

The civil noble lord's constitution is within the boundaries of science, which makes the civil noble lord legal, safe, and the differences between the civil and supernatural constitutions make the civil noble lord not criminally responsible. As a consequence supernatural beings are not allowed, directly or indirectly, to have political relationships with the civil noble lord. Political relationships imply that the civil noble lord is capable of criminal behaviour, are based on lies or role plays beyond the capabilities of the civil noble lord. Formality enforced by common law is necessary to protect the civil noble lord from the uncivilized unscientific constitutions of supernatural beings. When supernatural beings undermine this sacred determination governing their actions, they are trying to circumvent the security of the civil noble lord, for planned unlawful supernatural attacks on the civil noble lord.

SCIENCE

SCIENCE

Social science

SCIENCE

Social science is the understanding of the creation of the state or civilization and the relationships between beings within the state or civilization.

The failure of the state or civilization is reflected in social interactions or relationships.

For there to be life, social interactions or relationships, there has to be a successful creation of the state or civilization. The state is an extension of the civil noble lord, the civil rights and privileges of the civil noble lord form the legal framework or scientific process for the establishment of the state that regulates supernatural beings.

The nature of the supernatural constitution makes socialization impossible; the supernatural constitution is beyond the confines or boundaries of the state or civilization. The regulation of supernatural beings by the civil noble lord gives life to the supernatural constitution, aids supernatural beings in socialization or interaction.

The evidence confirms that the failure to constitute the state on this planet is as a consequence of the hostile nature of the supernatural constitution, the unregulated supernatural constitution. Supernatural beings are naturally hostile; tend only to thrive in hostile conditions and relationships hence the failure of socialization and the not constituted state. Supernatural beings unlawfully try to establish political relationships with the civil noble lord as if the civil noble lord is criminally responsible to breach the security of the civil rights of the civil noble lord to facilitate the failure of the state. This enables supernatural beings to maintain a lawless

SCIENCE

culture at the expense of constantly picking fights with the civil noble lord through relationships they established by force supernaturally beyond the capabilities of the civil noble lord. This is torturous for the civil noble lord, undermining the mental and physical wellbeing of the civil noble lord.
For the state to operate correctly there has to be a proper distinction between the scientific, natural and the unscientific, supernatural. Unfortunately, science is unlawfully being used as cover for the supernatural, unscientific which has a destabilizing effect on the state. Science is used to meet the needs of the civil scientific constitution, as a consequence when goods and services are unsafe or harmful to the legal scientific civil constitution they are unscientific and destabilizing to the state.
The United Kingdom passport was black, and was later changed to red, with pictures on the cover of the passport that are representations of the supernatural, a unicorn and a supernaturally altered lion with a crown. The pictures on the passport are contradictions to the state principle, the state that represents order, an extension of the scientific natural man.
It is a trait of the supernatural constitution, the supernatural ideology of nonexistence, to sabotage a need or necessity, to try to have you cornered for exploitation or prostitution, to be forced into their demonic gang. They do not seem to be aware that this is only possible if the target is criminally responsible, an unfortunate evidence of dumb criminal syndrome. The civil noble lord is a representation of god, the

SCIENCE

law. To attempt to have a representation of god cornered for demonic political purposes is criminal insanity, dumb criminal syndrome.

Science, social science, when applied correctly facilitates independence for civil and supernatural beings ensuring individual rights for all.

Science ensures that relationships are established correctly; it incorporates consent and regulation, to ensure civil beings are not used as toys to suit different supernatural political occasions and relationships are not forced on civil beings. It operates like a security sifting process to reveal supernatural criminals pretending to be law abiding but directly or indirectly party to the supernatural political lawless culture that persecutes the vulnerable including the civil noble lord. When supernatural beings try to establish relationships or connections supernaturally unlawfully with civil beings it is because they have fallen short of the necessary scientific standard as a consequence of criminal behaviour and have resorted to force. Being party to the lawless supernatural political persecutory culture is not compatible with submitting to the civil constitution as ruler or being law abiding.

The common law civil rights and privileges of the civil noble lord and the protocols for contact and communication with the civil noble lord by supernatural beings are scientific formulas that ensure consent and regulation.

International and domestic legislations only recognize the civil legal scientific constitution for the delivery of services as the standard for purposes of professionalism. To allow emotions to get in the way of the delivery of services by supernatural beings that develop personal relationships with the recipients of these services, in cases that the recipients do not know them, is a serious problem, and invites crimes of bullying, assault.

Parenting is a social science, which must have its foundation in an excellent understanding of the law, it is essential to identify, interpret, and apply the law correctly in order not to educate children incorrectly to become criminals and menaces to society.

Policing is a social science which must be achieved from a properly constituted police service, based on the truth of the existence of civil and supernatural beings. The truth makes governing uncomplicated, straightforward, without the need for politics or the need to have periodic elections. The resources for government are already in place, civil and supernatural beings, they only need to be applied correctly. Unfortunately, the current practice of policing based on lies with the different political factions of supernatural beings, the churches, synagogues, mosques, the not constituted police service, the political governments etcetera operating illegally, all have to be satisfied maintaining the status quo of lawlessness. When you have supernatural beings all wanting to be movers and shakers, power brokers, to have an important status in a lawless culture, a properly constituted state without the need for movers and shakers or power brokers, life will be boring for them even though they will be safe.

Organized fighting or organized crime the current political systems of government in the world, which is what these supernatural political factions represent, cater to the hostile nature of the supernatural constitution. Total anarchy is presented by these retarded supernatural beings as a type of social science.

The simplicity of the structure of the police service found in most countries, when properly constituted based on the reality of the existence of civil and supernatural beings, with the correct identification, interpretation, and application of the law, will be enough to govern or police the planet. This type of less government is sufficient to complement the resources already in existence, civil and supernatural beings. The United Nations is meant to be such a police service if the political structure is dismantled and reconstituted with a legal command structure.

The state represents order as an extension of the civil noble lord, supernatural manifestations as methods of identification or distinction are unlawful, chaotic. Order is the regulation of supernatural beings by the state. The distinction of supernatural beings with supernatural manifestations of wings for angels and horns for demons and other supernatural manifestations for supernatural animals contradict the state principle of order, the manifestations represent lawlessness.

The police service constituted correctly based on the truth of the existence of civil and supernatural beings is for keeping the peace. Peace is determined or defined using the civil noble lord as the standard, what is peaceful to one constitution might not be peaceful to another, the delicate nature of the civil noble lord makes the peace of the civil noble lord universal. The standard, the peace of the civil noble lord commissions the police. The police service properly constituted has a clear mandate, to maintain a way of life using the civil rights of the civil noble lord as the standard. Unlike the different supernatural political systems of government, whether it is a supernatural being unlawfully pretending to be a traditional ruler, or a military government of supernatural beings or political democratic governments of supernatural beings etcetera which are organized crimes, they are subject to change because of illegitimacy, a properly constituted police service is permanent because of legitimacy.

Less government is the dismantling of the unnecessary political structure within the current lawless supernatural political governments, especially within the United Nations, as a consequence of operating under the wrong identification, interpretation, and application of the law, making law enforcement impossible at the expense of the lives, physical and mental wellbeing of the vulnerable, including the civil noble lord. The dismantled political structure is replaced with a legal command structure operating under the correct identification, interpretation, and application of the law. The purpose of the police service is to keep the peace by the proper application of the

SCIENCE

resources already available, civil and supernatural beings, to preserve a predetermined way of life.

The undisciplined, unscientific nature of the supernatural constitution make it toxic, the need for the supernatural constitution to cater to its hyperactive nature creates toxic conditions. This means that for socialization to be possible it has to be militaristic, with the civil rights of the civil noble lord and the protocols for contact and communication with the civil noble lord as the legal framework or scientific process for socialization. For socialization to be possible it has to be based on the truth; there is a difference between lying to be a constitution you are not and behaving lawfully using the legal framework or scientific process for socialization as a guide. Lying aids supernatural beings to become destructive, self-harm, suicide, murder, organized crime or organized fighting etcetera.

The civil rights and privileges of the civil noble lord and the protocols for contact and communication with the civil noble lord are disability rights that redress the balance between the civil and supernatural constitutions with the sacred purpose of creating a civilization, law, and order.

These rights and privileges operate the same way the scientific invention the wheelchair operates for a crippled person, with the sacred effect in the case of the civil noble constitution of establishing law and order. Because of the constitution of the supernatural being these rights and privileges are taken for granted, pretending to be noble is not the same thing as being noble, supernatural beings cannot comprehend the need for the immediate implementation of these rights, privileges, and protocols. The things supernatural beings take for granted in their daily lives are only possible for the civil noble lord with the sacred wheelchair, the civil rights and privileges and the protocols for contact and communication. This means that the role of a real ruler is not elevation above your peers but to achieve equality which is then applied universally for the establishment and maintenance of the state or civilization. The police service that is properly constituted is a representation of the civil noble lord. The command structure within the police service is a representation of the civil noble lord. An example of this is when a supernatural sergeant issues a command to a constable; the sergeant is a representation of the civil noble lord, the real commissioner of police.

Science is being used unlawfully by supernatural beings to create problems, lawlessness, to create activities for themselves like diseases, war, at the expense of the peace of the vulnerable, at the expense of the peace of the civil noble lord.

The militaristic socialization or discipline of supernatural beings with the legal framework or scientific process of the civil rights and privileges of the civil noble lord and the protocols for contact and communication with the civil noble lord enable the scientification or ennoblement of supernatural beings. Any misapplication of the principle of the supremacy of the civil constitution will lead to total anarchy, organized butchery, or organized crime, given the undisciplined, unscientific nature of the supernatural constitution, the current practice at present.

There has always been an established order represented by Lord Adam in the science or Garden of Eden, which supernatural beings have rebelled against from its inception. Politics is revolutionary, revolution against an established order, rebellion against the civil scientific constitution, the standard. The political democratic systems of government are warfare disguised. The political system legalizes bullying or oppression or domination. The political system is the legalization of the compromise of a being or beings by another or others to have an advantage over them. The political systems of government, representations of the supernatural constitution, have introduced the political way of life to all aspects of daily life at present, disregard for the vulnerable, survival of the fittest. This madness is so enshrined in the psyche of the supernatural being that the being cannot comprehend the extent of their offensiveness. They believe that they can be friendly, within the boundaries of the political lawless culture, to the civil noble lord.

The market economy is an oppressive political capitalist system that breeds extreme discrimination that breeds total anarchy. The state economy on the other hand, the state capitalist system that uses the legality of real nobles, the nobility, to regulate supernatural beings, the working class, creates a fair system of equality given the differences between the civil and supernatural constitutions.

SCIENCE

The political supernatural system allows supernatural beings to unlawfully compromise the vulnerable, including the civil noble lord, different types of enslavement with the misuse of supernatural powers and senses for different types of emotional responses to cater to the sadistic needs of supernatural beings.

The social science concept has been misapplied by supernatural beings referred to as the social sciences for organized anarchy. It is used to create lawless systems to ensure that everyone falls below the required standard to be law abiding in order to be vulnerable to the unregulated interest from supernatural beings. To be susceptible to the lawless system you must be criminally responsible, a supernatural being. The supernatural ideology of nonexistence defines an angel as supernatural; the civil being who is already naturally righteous is deceived to aspire to be compromised to become an angel, to fit into the world of total anarchy. Otherwise the civil being will continue to be out of place, a threat to the world of total anarchy.

The state principle on the other hand is based on the civil noble lord being naturally righteous, already an angel with no supernatural manifestations, supernatural beings because of their supernatural powers and senses are required to behave appropriately with these supernatural powers and senses in order not to be disruptive or threats to the state to be regarded as law abiding or angels with no supernatural manifestations.

The European Union is an example of social science being

SCIENCE

used for obstruction rather than the construction of a civilization or state. The criteria to join the European Union are based on the lawless capitalist market economy rather than the state economy. Social science or policing is non-discriminatory, for construction rather than obstruction, and can only operate under the non-discriminatory state principle or economy. The poorer a territory or country the more assistance they need from a police service to construct a self-sustaining civilization. All territories or countries are areas covered by a legitimate police service; membership is automatic if the police service is legal and not political. The differences between the civil and supernatural constitutions confirm that the civil noble lord is incapable of lying; the differences also confirm that the civil noble lord is incapable of role plays; the civil noble lord goes into any situation in good faith. Lying and acting as a way of life is racist, not universal. This is the reality regardless of appearances and regardless of the civil rights of the civil noble lord, in particular the right to privacy.

SCIENCE

The supernatural unscientific constitution

SCIENCE

The supernatural constitution is beyond the boundaries of science, not within the legal and scientific definition of a human being or a person. This makes the supernatural constitution unscientific. The supernatural constitution has supernatural powers and senses. The unscientific nature of the supernatural constitution, the supernatural powers and senses, constitutes an unacceptable threat to the security, mental and physical wellbeing, of the scientific legal person recognized and protected by law.

The unscientific nature of the supernatural constitution is toxic, antisocial. This sacred determination was arrived at using the civil scientific constitution as the standard, measured against the delicate nature of the legally recognized civil noble lord.

The unscientific toxic nature of the supernatural constitution is reflected in relationships, communications, interests, methods, plans, solutions etcetera. Domestic and international legislations as a consequence do not permit supernatural beings any type of association with civil scientific legal beings, whether supernatural beings are pretending to be legal scientific beings or not, the supernatural constitution is not recognized by these legislations. Common law has gone as far as insisting on existing in different worlds or planets with very strict safeguards or guidelines or protocols when there is contact to protect the civil legal constitution from the unscientific hostile supernatural constitution.

The unscientific retarded nature of the supernatural

SCIENCE

constitution will result in the civil legal constitution being under constant unlawful supernatural attacks. The retardation will ensure that supernatural beings will make up any reason to subject the delicate civil scientific constitution to constant supernatural attacks. An objective assessment of the differences between the civil and supernatural constitutions will lead to the reasonable conclusion that the civil noble scientific constitution is not criminally responsible. The civil legal person is in any situation in good faith because of the lack of supernatural powers and senses.

The unscientific generic application of the civil noble lord by supernatural beings is as a puppet, object of ridicule, the civil noble lord open to the supernatural interest of all supernatural beings, automatic loss of the sacred civil right to privacy. Establishing relationships supernaturally, unregulated, by extremely dangerous beings are violations of the civil constitution's sacred right to life. The civilized generic legal application of the civil noble lord is as the standard, ruler, with the sacred civil rights, including the civil right to life and the civil right to privacy, integral to the application.

To be unscientific is to be stateless, which accounts for the real attitudes of supernatural beings to the state principle, the stateless ideology of the stateless constitution accounts for concern, help, solution, method, plan etcetera from the stateless constitution being poisonous, masks for statelessness.

The concept of the afterlife developed by supernatural

beings is statelessness, a reflection of the stateless nature of the supernatural constitution, complementary to the supernatural constitution and an unlawful compromise of the civil legal scientific constitution. The concept of the afterlife is totally unscientific, illogical, and racist when applied to the civil noble lord. The torturous concept has been developed for the punishment of the innocent, righteous civil lord, for not being wicked or unholy, who by nature rejects lawlessness or the unscientific.

The unfortunate reality is that supernatural beings believe that the distinction between supernatural beings, the angels, law abiding supernatural beings and the demons, criminals, are their physical appearances and their relationships with a supernatural being. The truth is that the civil scientific constitution is the standard by which supernatural beings are judged to be law abiding or criminals. The demons, criminals, are supernatural beings that undermine the authority of the civil noble lord, that compromise the civil noble lord in order to establish and maintain a lawless culture. The angels, the law abiding supernatural beings, are supernatural beings that uphold the law and operate under the authority of the civil noble lord as ruler, the standard.

Science, including social science is protection from statelessness. When supernatural beings establish connections or relationships supernaturally or unscientifically, the vulnerable including the civil noble lord is being drawn into statelessness. When the vulnerable are being stalked supernaturally or unscientifically, the sadism of trying to determine what the vulnerable can or cannot do every day, the vulnerable is being drawn into statelessness. When the vulnerable attracts the interest of supernatural beings, it means torturous existence for the vulnerable, being subjected to one form of anxiety after another, the life and health of the vulnerable always on the line, the vulnerable will constantly have the feeling of being forced into Russian roulette with the life of the vulnerable always on the line. These are the characteristics of the supernatural unscientific constitution.

The supernatural unscientific constitution is a representation of statelessness; unscientific methods of communication or interaction are aimed at compromising the state, the civil noble lord, to become stateless. The ghost has lost its scientific cohesion and has become unscientific, stateless. It is baffling that a constitution, the civil scientific constitution, who is not offensive, measured against the supernatural constitution, not criminally responsible, supernatural beings always look for an excuse to take offence at anything to justify compromising the civil noble lord, to turn the civil constitution stateless. It is like trying to get round landmines for the civil scientific constitution to have any sort of contact or interaction with supernatural beings, they take offence at anything to justify the unlawful misuse of supernatural powers to compromise the civil noble lord.

Anything is built up into a big or massive issue to justify compromising the civil noble lord, to unlawfully condemn the civil scientific constitution to statelessness. Diseases or

SCIENCE

illnesses, or ageing are forms of statelessness not associated with the state, the civil scientific constitution, but associated with the supernatural unscientific stateless constitution. Forgiveness is irrelevant with regard to the civil noble lord because the civil noble lord is not criminally responsible given the differences between the civil and supernatural constitutions, there is nothing to forgive. The stateless agenda of supernatural beings accounts for their unforgiving attitudes toward the civil noble lord, as if the civil noble lord is criminally responsible. Supernatural beings on the other hand are criminally responsible given their supernatural powers and senses which establish intent without a doubt; forgiveness is irrelevant for purposes of regulation and state security.

These are few of the reasons that domestic and international legislations do not permit supernatural beings contact and communication with the civil noble lord or civil beings. Common law in very limited situations permits contact and communication under very strict safeguards or guidelines for the protection of the delicate civil noble scientific lord, with the safeguards of the civil rights of the civil noble lord and the protocols for contact and communication with the civil noble lord.

The civil noble lord, the civil rights and privileges of the civil noble lord, the protocols for contact and communication with the civil noble lord, create the scientific process or legal framework that creates the state that regulate supernatural beings. This scientific regulation of supernatural beings

SCIENCE

transforms the unscientific supernatural being to a scientific sentient being. This transformation is achieved without the need for supernatural alterations or spells. The scientific process or legal framework enables socialization for supernatural beings. Proper lawful socialization is only possible with the ennoblement of supernatural beings.

The police services, the military service, the National Health Service are meant to be scientific services for the protection or security of the legal civil scientific person from real threats to the civil scientific rights of the civil scientific person. These services have been undermined or compromised by supernatural beings in favour of supernatural political lawless role plays that cater to the stateless nature of the unscientific stateless supernatural constitution at the expense of the security, physical and mental wellbeing of the civil scientific constitution. These compromises of the civil scientific rights of the civil scientific constitution constitute violations of the civil right to life contrary to article 3 of the universal declaration of human rights and article 6 of the international convention on civil and political rights. Crime prevention measures and healthcare provisions decreed for the legal person have been put on hold in favour of supernatural lawless stateless role plays. This means that these supernatural attacks, the police service, and the current healthcare provisions are crimes against the civil scientific constitution contrary to international law. Supernatural beings have given names to supernatural phenomena referred to as illnesses or diseases with varying recovery periods for different illnesses or diseases made possible by the controlled use of their supernatural powers and senses. These supernatural practices are violations of the civil scientific person's civil right to life and the civil right not to be tortured contrary to international law.

The sentience, intelligence, sanity, and morality of supernatural beings are linked to the civil scientific constitution, as the standard, they are dependent on how their actions affect the civil scientific constitution, man, the standard, the law.

The civil scientific constitution is a lifeboat, for true or real living, reinforced by the civil rights and privileges of the civil scientific constitution that form the the legal framework or scientific process for the creation of the state or civilization. The supernatural unscientific beings have conjured up the unlawful conception of morality within the context or boundaries of lawlessness, the lawless culture their creation, a representation of the the lawless stateless lifeless supernatural unscientific constitution. Their creation of right and wrong within the boundaries or confines of the lawless culture similar to the Nazis' creation of right and wrong within the occupied territories that were forced on the people within those territories. The civil scientific constitution has the misfortune to attract the misplaced goodwill of demons, supernatural unscientific beings that want to fit the civil scientific constitution into their concept of good or right supernaturally within the lawless culture they created. These are the symptoms of the dumb criminal syndrome unique to supernatural beings, extreme retardation.

SCIENCE

SCIENCE

The civil scientific constitution

SCIENCE

The civil scientific constitution, commonly referred to as man, is a being within the scientific description of a person or human being, without supernatural powers and senses. This scientific being needs the scientific environment, scientific methods, scientific behaviour from others to function, and for security and independence.

The civil scientific constitution naturally rejects, or is repulsed by, the supernatural unscientific constitution, naturally allergic; socialization with the unscientific supernatural constitution is beyond the capabilities of the civil scientific constitution.

Comprehensibility, clarity of information and communication, in a scientific legal way given the differences between the civil and supernatural constitutions, is essential for regulation and state security. It is important to understand that the standard for clarity or comprehensibility is the civil legal scientific constitution.

The unscientific, toxic nature of the supernatural constitution makes an open relationship with the civil scientific constitution unlawful, harmful to the civil scientific constitution. The supernatural powers and senses of the supernatural constitution make the supernatural constitution criminally responsible, there is the possibility of criminal behaviour, so relationships with supernatural beings cannot be open but closed because supernatural beings must be regulated. The only general application of the civil noble lord is as the standard, regulator, with the right to life and the right to privacy integral to the application.

SCIENCE

The civil scientific constitution is the civilization or metropolitan police service, whose legal needs establish the state that regulates supernatural beings. The racist nature of the supernatural constitution cannot comprehend the absolute authority of the civil scientific constitution; the nature of the barbarian is to equate authority with the strength to fight or to challenge your opponents as the right of authority to govern which maintains lawlessness.

The civil scientific constitution as the representation of the police service is the commissioner of police, the distinction as commissioner also implies nobility, in the case of a real noble it is confirmation of not being criminally responsible, and integrity. This sacred distinction has been misapplied, undermined by supernatural beings unlawfully pretending to be of civil scientific constitutions dishonestly presented as commissioners of police. The sacred distinction protects the civil scientific constitution from the conspiratorial attitudes of supernatural beings to collectively undermine the effectiveness of the law, to establish lawless conditions that suit their hostile constitutions. Supernatural beings are criminally responsible, there is always the possibility of criminal behaviour, and only those responsible for undermining the police service as a consequence of criminal behaviour should be affected by the appropriate punishment, which could include dismissal.

Science is an extension of the civil scientific constitution, which is used to meet the scientific legal needs of the civil scientific constitution, goods, and services must meet the criteria of usability, accessibility, durability, and safety using the civil scientific constitution as the standard. Unfortunately, the current practice is the use of supernatural beings pretending to be civil beings to determine the suitability of goods and services making them unlawfully toxic for the civil scientific constitution. In some situations that goods and services provide a degree of assistance for the civil scientific constitution like healthcare including physical fitness they are sabotaged, obstructed turning a little scientific legal protection and independence to full blown political dependency for attention and worship. This is especially the case when they are legitimately rejected for their extreme wickedness.

The civil scientific constitution can only establish communications, contacts, relationships, or associations in a civilized legal scientific way, supernatural connections, relationships etcetera with the civil scientific constitution are unlawful, forbidden. The nature of the supernatural constitution is as such that connections, relationships, contacts, communications etcetera must be regulated and consented to by the civil scientific constitution. Common law has provided safeguards or guidelines that ensure regulation and consent. The current practice of two or more friends having a casual conversation or joke about something, because one of the friends is a supernatural being, he or she torments or tortures the others everyday of their lives supernaturally because of a casual conversation or joke that did not involve the use of supernatural powers and senses.

This is even more bizarre when no friendship exist but a supernatural connection forced on the vulnerable, an individual is alone but has to live life as if navigating landmines because of forced supernatural relationships beyond the capabilities of the civil scientific constitution. The barring of supernatural relationships, connections etcetera is reinforced by international and domestic legislations, common law, the civil rights, and privileges of the civil scientific constitution and the protocols for contact and communication.

Supernatural beings are mesmerized or intoxicated by their supernatural powers and senses, the dazzling effect will not work on another supernatural being, so the civil scientific constitution that they are forbidden to subject to the display of their supernatural abilities, magical show, is the only attraction for the dazzling effect at the expense of serious mental and physical harm. This takes the form of constant daily stalking with different types of spells on the civil scientific constitution.

Because supernatural beings choose to self-destruct through suicide pacts, or deliberate destructive criminal behaviour, or political role plays while pretending to be civil beings does not mean that these self-destructive lifestyles can be forced on real civil beings. The lifespan of the civil scientific constitution has been determined to be indefinite or immortality and should look young and good. I will estimate that the intention was for the civil scientific constitution not to look older than twenty four years. The lesson in the

Garden of Eden was that Lord Adam lost the right to immortality not as a civil scientific being but as a supernatural being. The civil scientific constitution is incapable of criminal behaviour.

The intention was for the individual to determine his or her lifespan and not for others to determine directly or indirectly. The civil scientific constitution requires scientific living conditions which are established and maintained by social scientific components, which are the civil rights and privileges of the civil scientific constitution, the protocols for contact and communication with the civil scientific constitution. These social scientific components or elements assist supernatural beings to socialize or interact with each other. Supernatural beings do not need to be humiliated or dehumanized for the process of socialization or interaction by lying or acting because of the nature of the supernatural constitution. These social scientific elements or components construct a scientific method of communication that respects or protects individual rights without the need to act or lie. These civil scientific rights, like the right to life, the right to self-determination, the right to privacy, freedom from torture, freedom of expression etcetera, assist supernatural beings to interact or socialize with each other individually or as individuals given the unscientific nature of the supernatural constitution, under the dominion or authority of the civil scientific constitution.

Saboteurs of science distinguish between the unscientific and scientific, by making the determination that the scientific is a

SCIENCE

slower process. The real distinction is the cost to your mental and physical wellbeing, the price of association with the unscientific. The scientific can be very quick as the unscientific or magical, the difference is safety, accessibility, freedom or independence, durability, orderliness, the dignity of person, freedom from worship, freedom from being stalked supernaturally etcetera.

There is nothing contentious about the concepts of science, governance, rules, and ruler; they are sacred types of disability rights for man that has wider sacred regulatory applications. The contention is the undermining of these sacred concepts, their misappropriation or sabotage by those they are meant to regulate. They are used by the wicked to persecute man. The credibility of these sacred concepts has been compromised by their misuse or misapplication.

The civil scientific constitution has to be distinguished from the supernatural unscientific constitution as ruler, as is required by law. The distinction must be done scientifically, legally and not unscientifically, supernatural, politically. The rights of the civil scientific constitution are legal and not political; these rights are not dependent on the mood swings of supernatural beings.

SCIENCE

SCIENCE

Author's notes

SCIENCE

My book science, explores the concept of science, its relationship with the law. It examines the redefinition and reapplication of science to cater to the wicked nature of the supernatural being. It examines the use of science for racist purposes, to persecute the vulnerable, contradictions of its primary purpose, the liberation of the vulnerable.

The film, fight club, fiction, with actors Brad Pitt and Edward Norton, is about illegal fighting, people that like to fight each other with no rules. They, the participants, do not talk about fight club. They fight each other, viciously inflicting pain on each other. The lawless unscientific culture is like the fight club, agreements between supernatural beings to establish and maintain this way of life. If you live by the sword, you die by the sword agreement. This requires a supernatural conspiracy to establish and maintain inhumane or inhospitable unscientific living conditions.

Given the differences between the civil scientific and the supernatural unscientific constitutions, the civil scientific constitution is incapable of giving offence, as a consequence cannot be party to such racist persecutory agreements. The civil scientific constitution can only function under hospitable scientific living conditions.

Death, illness or disease, ageing are supernatural unscientifically phenomena self-inflicted either as punishments for criminal behaviour or because of self-destructive role plays, both role plays and criminal behaviour are beyond the capabilities of the civil scientific constitution. This implies that the supernatural constitution has a choice,

SCIENCE

which should be extended to the civil scientific constitution. Naturally, the supernatural constitution will choose to self-harm, the civil scientific constitution will not choose to self-harm.

Science, the state, the civil scientific constitution provide the necessary economy or restrictions, given the nature of the supernatural constitution, to make living in the right scientific conditions possible. It is only the civil scientific constitution that can make the right determination about the necessary economy or restrictions needed for the right scientific living conditions. The unscientific supernatural being, unlawfully pretending to be a scientific being, will undoubtedly redefine, and misapply the scientific principle of economy or restrictions for racist persecutory purposes.

The hostile nature of the supernatural constitution, the possibility of criminal behaviour, as a consequence of supernatural powers and senses, regardless of the supernatural being, require that relationships or continued relationships with civil scientific beings are dependent on good behaviour or being law abiding.

After becoming aware of the differences between the civil and supernatural constitutions that were concealed from me for decades at the expense of physical and mental abuse, I have re-educated myself based on the truth of the differences between the civil and supernatural constitutions. The education is based on the true constitutions of those around me, supernatural constitutions.

The process that led to the establishment of the United

Nations, the invasion of Poland, the occupation of France, the extermination of the Jews, etcetera by the Nazis confirm that although the Nazis provided some degree of security, healthcare etcetera in these occupied territories they were nevertheless considered an oppressive illegitimate government.

Illegitimate, oppressive governments introduce torture, mental and physical abuse of the vulnerable, as a way of life, characteristics of the supernatural constitution, precisely what a legitimate police service is meant to eliminate.

Science is an extension of the civil scientific constitution that bridges the gap between the civil and supernatural constitutions; the bridge creates the state or civilization that regulates the supernatural unscientific constitution ennobling the supernatural unscientific constitution.

The independence, freedom and security of science rather than the enslavement, toxicity, dependency and worship of the unscientific make science the law.

Science, given the differences between the civil and supernatural constitutions, is militarization, to make everything safe.

The confidence of the supernatural unscientific being is false confidence, linked to the unscientific perceptions of the unscientific supernatural constitution, responsible for the lawless stateless unscientific culture, the unlawful persecution of the vulnerable. It is a recipe for disaster. Insanity should not be mistaken for confidence. The guidance of the law, the civil scientific being, is crucial to the civilized

SCIENCE

development of supernatural beings, domestication.

As a civil being, all my life to date, I have been constantly under different types of supernatural spells, spells of alterations to my body, spells of misinformation or deception or lies, spells of mind control, spells of compromises or violations of my civil rights and privileges. These civil rights and privileges are sacred types of disability rights for the civil being given the differences between the civil and supernatural constitutions. Relationships or associations or agreements with civil beings are not possible or cannot be consented to without these civil scientific rights and privileges to bridge the gap between the civil and supernatural constitutions.

Supernatural beings cannot claim relationships or associations or agreements or expect to establish relationships or associations or agreements with the victims of their spells especially during the period of the spell or spells. This is similar in principle to contract law; contracts are void if entered into under duress, an altered mental state.

A legal scientific system of government takes everyone's needs seriously and makes adequate provisions, and a political unscientific system of government only considers the needs of the political class, supernatural beings, and is a discriminatory racist system that disregards the needs of those they consider weak, without political influence, civil scientific beings.

Supernatural beings have the ability to stave off supernatural

SCIENCE

attacks from their peers, like spells etcetera, giving them a choice, science in the form of a properly constituted police service gives the vulnerable including the civil scientific constitution a choice. The right to choose does not exist for the vulnerable at present because of the lack of a properly constituted police service. So spells are removed from the vulnerable only by the goodwill of the wicked keeping the vulnerable at the mercy of the wicked in a lawless culture. This accounts for why spells put on the vulnerable in a lawless culture go on indefinitely, not removed.

Author's biography

SCIENCE

My name is Lord Loveday Ememe. I was born in the United Kingdom and of African origin. I am a graduate of an Anglican seminary school. I graduated from the University of East London with an honours degree in law. I am of a civil scientific constitution.

Bibliography

SCIENCE

The Bible

SCIENCE

www.ingramcontent.com/pod-product-compliance
Lightning Source LLC
Chambersburg PA
CBHW070432180526
45158CB00017B/982